Horus the Misunderstood Buzzard

Tid-Bit Has a Secret

By Mary Deborah Bowden

© 2023

ISBN #:   978-0-9968677-0-2

Illustrations by: Sanghamitra Dasgupta

This Book Belongs to:

_____

Mission statement:

The *Horus the Misunderstood Buzzard* series is geared for the 5 to 7 year old and is suitable for home schooling. As the books are separate stories rather than a continuation, they can be read in any order.

Reading comprehension/opinion questions and vocabulary are included. Bright pictures hold the reader's attention and aid understanding as loving characters help each other solve various personal problems.

Horus, the Misunderstood Buzzard: Tid-Bit Has a Secret

Written by
Deborah Bowden

Illustrated by
Sanghamitra Dasgupta

Acknowledgements

I would like to thank my daughter, Erin Bradleigh Bowden for her invaluable contribution to the Horus series.
We make a great team.

I would also like to thank my illustrator, Sanghamitra Dasgupta, for bringing Horus and his friends to life.

Chapter 1
Flying

Horus and Giblet go flying everyday. Several animals ask Horus to take them flying. He says, "No. I can only fly little animals. You're too heavy."

Stanley raccoon says, "I'm little; fly me." Ellie opossum says, "I'm little; fly me." Ralph rabbit says, "I'm little; fly me." They all climb on his back.

Giblet can't see Horus. He's under the three animals.
"Help," says Horus.

3

Giblet climbs on the pile and
tickles Stanley, Ellie, and Ralph.

They giggle and wiggle and fall off.

Giblet says, "Only mice, rats, chipmunks, and squirrels are small enough to fly with Horus."

Horus says, "We should ask Tid-Bit if he'd like to fly with us."

Chapter 2
Tid-Bit's Secret

Horus and Giblet fly to Tid-Bit's short, hollow tree. Tid-Bit is in his garden.

Horus asks, "Tid-Bit, would you like to fly with us?"

"No!" Tid-Bit says, "I'm afraid of heights. That's why I live in a short tree."

Giblet and Horus are surprised. "You're a squirrel. Squirrels climb very tall trees and walk on branches. Why didn't you tell us?" Giblet asks.

Tid-Bit tucks his head. "If other squirrels find out, they will make fun of me and say mean things.

I tell them I live here because of my garden. They don't know. Please don't tell."

8

Horus says, "You're our friend. Giblet and I will never tell your secret. Maybe I can help you."

"How can you help me? My short tree is almost too high. When I look down, my head spins. I get weak," Tid-Bit says.

Chapter 3
Horus Helps

"Climb on my back, and I will fly down to the ground," Horus says.

Tid-Bit is afraid, but he trusts Horus.
He climbs on.

Horus slowly circles down, down, down. He reaches the ground. Tid-Bit is afraid.

"I will fly back up to my branch by your garden. You climb up to me. We will fly back down again."

12

Tid-Bit climbs up to meet Horus,
and they fly down again.
Tid-Bit is not too afraid this time.

They do this over
and over again.
Tid-Bit isn't afraid
any more.
He thinks it's fun.

13

"Now," Horus says, "Stay on my back and I will fly up to my branch."

Tid-Bit is afraid, but not too afraid.

Horus flies up, and back down, and then back up. Tid-Bit is having fun. They go up and down over and over.

Then Horus says,
"Hold on tight.
I will fly to that
other tree,
but I will stay
down low."

Tid-Bit isn't afraid.
Horus flies to another
tree, and then to another.

15

Soon Horus is flying
Tid-Bit all around
the open field.

He flies just above
Stanley's, Ralph's, and
Ellie's heads.

They run and hide.
"Too fast, too low," they yell..

16

Chapter 4
The Squirrels
Watch

Squirrels high up in the trees
watch Horus and Tid-Bit fly.

They run over when Horus and
Tid-Bit land. They ask
Tid-bit, "Why do you fly
so low?"

18

Tid-Bit doesn't know what to say. He's afraid they know his secret.

Horus wants to protect his friend.

He remembers what Stanley, Ralph, and Ellie said.

He says, "It's much harder to fly low. I have to fly very fast or I'll crash.

Tid-Bit likes to go very fast and very low. He likes to watch the ground rush by."

Frank squirrel says, "I don't believe you. I think Tid-Bit is afraid to go higher. Maybe that's why he lives in a short tree.

Show me it's harder. I want to go fast and low."

He climbs on Horus.

20

Horus flies as low and as fast as he can.
He can't let the other squirrels know
Tid-Bit's secret.

Frank looks down. The ground is very close.
It rushes by so fast that Frank is very, very afraid.
His head spins, and he is weak.

"Stop, help, get me off," he screams.

"Tid-Bit is the bravest of all squirrels."

Now Tid-Bit goes flying every day. He and Giblet take turns.

None of the squirrels or other animals *ever* ask to fly with Horus. They aren't as brave as Tid-Bit.

The End

Reading Comprehension and Opinion Questions with Answers

Tid-Bit Has a Secret

On the next page are possible questions that can be used to gauge a child's understanding of the story, if so desired; a few require a child's opinion. Some or all may be asked or others substituted. This is NOT a test.

1. **What is Tid-Bit's problem?**

   Accept: He's afraid of heights.

   Opinion, possible answers: He's a squirrel and squirrels aren't supposed to be afraid of heights, he's afraid other squirrels will make fun of him if they know his secret, other squirrels won't like him, they'll stay away from him, he'll be different, they might bully him.

2. **How do Giblet and Horus find out Tid-Bit's secret?**

   Accept: They ask him to go flying.

   Opinion, possible answer: Tid-Bit trusts his friends and tells them.

3. **How is Horus a good friend? Accept: He flies Tid-Bit up and down until he isn't afraid, he helps Tid-Bit enjoy flying, he flies low to the ground.**

   Opinion, possible answers: Horus will never tell Tid-Bit's secret, He defends Tid-Bit against Frank squirrel, he always flies low so Tid-Bit won't be afraid, he remembers what Ellie, Ralph, and Stanley say and gets an idea to help Tid-Bit, he flies very fast to scare Frank so he'll believe Tid-Bit is brave.

4. What does Frank squirrel think?

Opinion, possible answers: He thinks Tid-Bit is afraid of heights, he doesn't believe that Tid-Bit likes to go fast, he wants Horus to prove Tid-Bit isn't afraid, he thinks Horus is lying, he thinks he can bully Tid-Bit

5. What do Frank and the other squirrels think after Horus gives Frank a ride?

Accept: Tid-Bit is very brave, Tid-Bit is the bravest squirrel around.

Opinion, possible answers: The squirrels will never believe Tid-Bit is afraid of heights again, is a hero, he's the best of all the squirrels, they admire Tid-Bit, no other animals will fly with Horus so they won't find out Tid-Bit's secret.

Vocabulary

These words are for older grades.
Do you know what they mean?

Opossum (3rd grade)   Heights (4th grade)

Hollow (3rd grade)   Protect (4th grade)

www.ingramcontent.com/pod-product-compliance
Lightning Source LLC
LaVergne TN
LVHW072056070426

835508LV00002B/123